The V

By Annette Smith
Photographs by Lindsay Edwards

Our family has a little dog.
His name is Scamp.

Scamp is not very well.
Mum and I are taking him
to the vet.
The vet is an animal doctor.

VET
OPEN
PORT PHILLIP

We go into the **clinic** with Scamp.
Mum talks to the vet nurse.

I look after Scamp.
He sits next to me.

We have to wait here
for the vet.

The vet comes to get us.
We go into her room.
She helps me put Scamp
onto a table.

The vet pats Scamp,
and talks to him.

First, the vet checks
Scamp's hair and skin.

Scamp does not look happy.
His eyes are big and sad.
His tail is down, too.

The vet has a **stethoscope**.
She puts it on Scamp's side.

Scamp does not like it.
He moves around.

The vet pats him.
She wants him to stay very still.

The vet looks inside Scamp’s ears
with a little **light.**
She says that his ears are clean.
There are no bugs in them.

She checks his eyes, too.

Next, the vet looks at Scamp's teeth.
She says that his **gums** are red.
They will be sore.

The vet shows us some dog food
that will help Scamp get better.
She wants to check him
again next week.

Dental Care
t/d

Glossary

clinic

gums

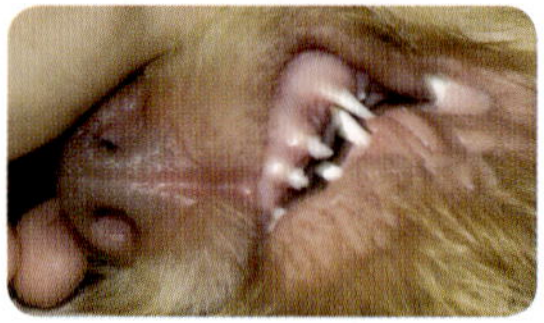

light

stethoscope

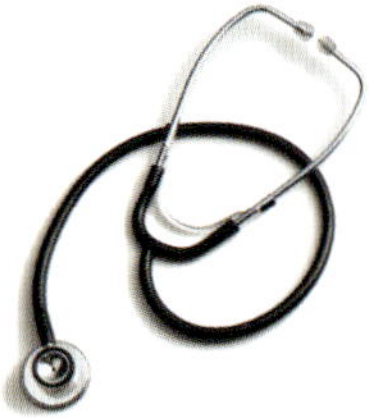